Autism, Bullying and Me

AUTISM, BULLYING AND ME

The Really Useful Stuff You Need to Know About Coping Brilliantly with Bullying

Emily Lovegrove

Jessica Kingsley Publishers
London and Philadelphia

First published in 2020
by Jessica Kingsley Publishers
73 Collier Street
London N1 9BE, UK
and
400 Market Street, Suite 400
Philadelphia, PA 19106, USA
www.jkp.com

Library of Congress Cataloging in Publication Data
A CIP catalog record for this book is available from the Library of Congress

British Library Cataloguing in Publication Data
A CIP catalogue record for this book is available from the British Library

ISBN 978 1 78775 213 9
eISBN 978 1 78775 214 6

Printed and bound in Great Britain

CONTENTS

CONTENTS

ACKNOWLEDGMENTS

My huge thanks to everyone at Jessica Kingsley
Publishers – to typesetters, designers, proofreaders;
to Karina Maduro who kindly guided me through
the publishing process; and to Andrew James who
commissioned one book, patiently waited...and then
accepted this different book instead (I promise I'll
write the book you wanted, for parents, next)!

Phenomenal thanks to teenagers Oriel Gray and Miles
Owen who read my drafts, made helpful suggestions
and were hugely, heart-warmingly enthusiastic.

And the fabulous army of autistic Twitter people who
encouraged all the way through.

I'm grateful always to all those school students who

contributed to the original research by experimenting and documenting with me.

And lastly, to Chris Lovegrove, Cameron Lovegrove, Bea Lovegrove-Owen and Susan Hodgkinson, who never fail to encourage and support – a massive thank you.

INTRODUCTION

Being different in some way can be extremely scary, especially if you're a teenager.

Add in bullying...aargh. Horrible word. Even the sound is brutal.

So, this will be a depressing book, right?

Nope, absolutely, totally wrong!

This will be a massively positive book.

We'll first do the science bit and look at what people say is 'normal' (yet another hateful word) and how that might affect us.

Then we'll look at what people *say* about bullying and

how that can be totally different to what *actually* happens.

Finally, we'll look at some self-empowering strategies on how to deal with all that 'being different' and sorting out bullying stuff so that we feel hugely better about ourselves.

So definitely a positive book!

Ready?

Oops! Just realised I never did that thing you're supposed to do when you meet someone – introduce yourself... I'm Emily. I'm a psychologist (I study how our brains affect how we behave – it's *totally* interesting) and a mum and a granny. I love wild spaces and animals, especially horses.

I feel a bit awkward because I'm writing this book for you and I don't actually know your name. But I'm imagining you as someone who is around 10 to 16 – maybe older – and I am really, *really* pleased to meet you. 😊

Chapter 1

AM I NORMAL?

Right, let's tackle this bit first because it's probably the thing most teens worry about.

The Oxford English Dictionary describes normal as 'conforming to a standard; usual, typical or expected'.

So, **are YOU normal**?

The short answer is **YES, YOU ARE**.

The longer answer is: 'We might not be what is expected but this just means that in some ways we are different.' And that's a positive, not a negative thing. I'll explain...

We'll look at our appearance first, as an example.

Normal just means 'average'. For instance, normal (average) height for adult males is around 176cm in the UK, and for women it's 161cm.

Neither is an *ideal*. They are just average 'normal' heights.

And normal (average) weight for Asian adult males is 57 kilos. But it's 80 kilos in North America.

Again, you can easily see that neither is an ideal, perfect weight. They are just an average of all male weights in specific countries.

Over the years, doctors and scientists have measured every part of us and come up with a rough average.

This is really handy if, for instance, you need an operation. The amount of anaesthetic used will depend on your weight. Too little anaesthetic for your weight won't knock you out; too much will knock you out for longer than is necessary.

Does that make more sense? I can't say this loudly enough; I'll need to shout:

NORMAL MEANS AVERAGE!

What's hard is when we feel we don't *look* average. Because then we feel we stand out as different and we feel self-conscious.

What about if you're extra tall, extra short, fatter than average, thinner than average, wear specs, have spots, wear different clothes or have a different skin colour from most people around you? What if you just feel you don't look the way you want to look?

You may not be average. *But you are definitely still normal!*

And just in case no one's ever explained this to you, it's also really important to remember that as teens you have what's called 'asymmetric growth'. This means when you have that teenage growth spurt – anywhere between, on average, 10 and 19 years – your feet and hands grow first. Then your arms and legs. And finally, your body. NO WONDER you can feel awkward and clumsy! And hormones are just a whole other complication!

But what if you were born with any condition that made your features different from others (like Down syndrome or cleft lip) or you've got scars from surgery for cancer, or for burns, or from an accident?

You may not be 'average' either. *But YOU are still absolutely normal!*

It's simply that some of your features might fall outside those measurements for average.

What is extra difficult in this case is that if you look different in any way, others are going to notice you. For instance, most people are able to walk. If you're in a wheelchair, you will attract extra attention because it's different from that 'normal' (average) method of walking.

And it's exactly the same if you have a different skin tone or wear different clothing from the average person in your area. People will notice you more.

They make decisions about you based on bits of (often totally inaccurate) information they've heard somewhere...

Have you heard of stereotyping? This is when people hear something about one or two people in a group that's different from their own group...and then decide *everyone* in that other group is the same.

It's stupid when you look at it like that, isn't it?

But now you know, you can understand that we all need to fight hard against doing this sort of simple and unfair way of judging others.

☆ **What about your sexuality? What if you are LGBT+?**

It's not very long, historically, since it was definitely regarded as *ab*normal to be anything other than heterosexual. And in some countries, it is still a criminal offence to be anything other than this. We must hope that this changes because it may not be the *average*, but it is *definitely* normal. You have the right to be exactly who you are.

What if you are autistic/have ADHD (attention deficit hyperactivity disorder)/OCD (obsessive compulsive behaviour)/Tourette's and you behave differently from most people around you because

of difficulties with processing information and emotions? Or maybe you are extremely sensitive to noise, light, touch, taste or smell? Or you might stim (use soothing repetitive actions to calm yourself down)? And what if you have some mental health difficulty such as depression, which makes it very hard to engage with others?

You might not be made to feel normal either. But you definitely ARE! You're just not 'average'.

In this case, you are 'differently wired', which means your brain works really well in its own way, but in different ways from the average.

Yep, there may well be things that complicate life such as being uncertain about which emotion you are feeling (alexithymia) or exactly where your arms and legs are (proprioception) or struggling to sequence letters or sentences (dyslexia). Not recognising faces can be another problem (prosopagnosia).

It used to be thought that all autistics have communication difficulties. What we're finding, more and more, is that we simply communicate *differently* from the average person. We can usually communicate with each other perfectly well!

And remember there is often an ability to focus intently on something you're interested in, and also to think creatively and unusually to come up with an original solution to problems that can defeat the 'average' person.

And if you look at it like that – normal just means average – then do you really, really want your life to be 'just average'?

You might not feel it right at this moment, but wouldn't you rather be a unique, amazing, creative, inspiring person?

Why do we cling on to this idea of 'normal' as being so desirable?

What we really mean is we want to fit in with others. We need other people to like us because we instinctively know that this is safer than being a 'loner'.

So, you will tend to be friendly with people who are similar to you. Who like the same things, who look sort of familiar. Who communicate and behave mostly like you.

And you will take longer to recognise, or be friendly towards, someone who looks or behaves differently from you.

Again, this is just average behaviour, based on years of evolution. It's the way 'average' brains are wired – to spot differences and check out if other people might be a threat to us. It might seem like a negative thing, but being initially cautious about people you don't know is actually a very good thing.

Where autistic teens (and I include myself here as an autistic adult) differ in this 'being cautious about others' is that often we have a tendency to take people at face value. Sometimes this is not a good thing as we can be a bit naïve about other people's motives in being friendly towards us. But other times it's brilliant because we have amazing conversations or friendships with the most unlikely and interesting people!

I read a brilliant book once by an author called Jeanette Winterson, whose mother said to her, 'Why be happy when you could be normal?'

What do you think about that? Would you honestly prefer to be normal/average/ordinary rather than be happy?

I don't know about you, but to me it makes absolutely no sense! How can I be really happy if I have to spend my life pretending to be something I'm not? What we all really want is to be loved *for who we ARE*!

But before I finish banging on about being average, can I ask you to please, please remember:

There is absolutely nothing to stop you from finding out more about someone who is different from you, so that you develop knowledge and understanding of all the diverse, fantastic varieties of 'normal but not average' people who exist on our planet.

It makes you much, MUCH more confident when you can see that there is a reason for their differences. And best of all is when you realise that negotiating those differences is massively better for all of us than just fighting them, regardless of who gets hurt.

I also need to tell you here that at the end of this book I've given you a list of useful organisations that were set up specifically to help each group. They can give you all sorts of details about different stuff that might be worrying you. And, importantly, opportunities to meet others who are like you.

Phew! Now we've got that first bit sorted out, we'll get on to the bit about what bullying is and whether what people *say* about it is true or just plain wrong (fake news)!

Chapter 2

WHAT IS 'BULLYING'?

(FACTS AND FAKE NEWS)

This is another minefield!

There is NO legal definition of what bullying is, but schools have a legal obligation to have an anti-bullying policy. What most tend to say is something along the lines of:

Bullying is a repeated intention to hurt someone either physically or emotionally. It is often aimed at certain groups, for example because of race, religion, gender or sexual orientation.

This is a good start at a definition. But I'm sure you, like me, can already see problems with it...

Repeated: What happens if somebody was really foul to you just the once? What if they said something really upsetting and you then felt extremely angry? Or really, really scared and anxious?

Did you not definitely still feel bullied?

Intentional: Well, sometimes people just say weird and stupid and ill-informed things. They don't necessarily *mean* to bully anyone.

But if you've been the butt of a stupid joke that makes you feel completely humiliated, don't you still feel bullied?

The difficulty here is that it doesn't matter whether the bullying was intentional or repeated. If you *feel* bullied, it has *exactly* the same effect on you as if someone came up and thumped you hard for no reason except that they 'felt like it'.

Important fact...

You will *still* feel threatened. You will *still* feel stressed, your body *still* reacts by making sure you breathe shallowly, and your digestion *still* stops working so well.

Worst of all, all your energy is directed to your arms and legs in case you have to fight, or run away, and there is less oxygen going to your brain so you can't even think clearly.

So some of the things people say about bullying aren't quite right!

It would be useful to look at some of the other myths (the fake news) around bullying so we're absolutely clear about what we mean, and how that affects how we might feel about it.

BULLYING MAKES YOU STRONGER!

Fact or fake news?

Definitely fake news. Bullying does *not* make you stronger, however much people say it.

Some people manage to *overcome* awful bullying and go on to be successful. That's brilliant.

But for most people, their self-esteem goes right down – they stop believing the world is a magical place. They feel a lot weaker.

BULLIES ARE EVIL!

More fake news.

The thing is, we all grow up wanting to feel good about ourselves.

Some do it in positive ways – they do well at sport, or reading, or helping others. To be successful at feeling good this way takes a lot of time and practice.

Some do it in negative ways – by putting others down (so that they feel superior). To be successful, this takes an awful lot of time and practice too...

Same goal, very different approaches!

Sometimes people choose the positive way and sometimes the negative way. The more you choose one way over the other, the more of a habit it becomes. And the more skilled you become.

So, if you've learnt the negative way, have practised hard and are successful, it's going to be hard to give that up, isn't it?

Understanding this idea of how people work to feel good about themselves is going to stand you in good stead when we get to sorting out bullying later on in the book.

IT WAS JUST A JOKE!

Most people think this is true. But again, it's actually *fake news*.

When people make fun of you in public, you might just scowl. But often what people do is what's called 'an appeasing gesture'. This means you do subconsciously recognise that what was said was a sort of threat, but also that it would be difficult or impossible to retaliate (fight back in some way), especially with everyone looking on. And you feel really embarrassed about that. So you grin. Or even laugh.

And now it seems you have no defence. You say you were upset and felt bullied. Everyone else says, 'But it was only a joke! And you were laughing!'

Complicated, isn't it? We'll need strategies for that too.

IGNORE BULLIES AND THEY'LL STOP!

Hmm. More complications. *More fake news.*

Logically, if you don't give bullies the satisfaction of reacting to whatever they said or did, it's very possible they will leave you alone.

But they may also just try harder...

The important thing to recognise here is that when we feel bullied, a whole set of physical things happens because that feeling of being bullied is *stressful*:

1. Your heart rate goes up, your breathing becomes shallow, your digestion stops!

2. Worse still, your energy goes *away* from your brain (so it's almost impossible to think clearly) and into your arms and legs so that you can either fight or run away (or you might just freeze up).

So, you can see that 'Just ignoring the bullying' in *physical* terms – what's happening to your body and brain – is never, ever successful, is it?

No problem. I'll show you other, actually successful

ways of dealing with this piece of 'Just ignore it!' fake news presently.

FIGHT BACK AND THEY'LL STOP!

Yet more complications.

Suppose someone thumps you really hard for no reason except they felt like doing it? You know you'll be in trouble if you fight back. Or maybe you just think this is a stupid way to behave? Anyway, they keep doing it and eventually you decide you've had enough. You thump them back. Really hard.

This can go one of three ways.

1. **Possible:** They are shocked and learn new respect for you. They definitely leave you alone in future.

2. **More likely:** They get their mates involved and they join in with the thumping.

3. **Probable:** Whether it was Way 1 or Way 2 above, you are the one who gets caught doing the thumping. You are now the one in trouble at school, at home, possibly even with the police...

And what if you are not someone who can – or wants to – fight back? What if you're the kind of person whose instinct tells them it's actually safer to run away?

Or if you are the kind of person who, when threatened or hurt, simply freezes?

Clearly, we're going to need good, strong strategies for dealing with this bit of 'Just fight back' fake news!

JUST TELL SOMEONE!

The idea here is that you tell an adult and they sort it out and everything is fine. They say things like 'If you don't tell us, how can we possibly help you?'

Simple!

No, really NOT simple. For several reasons:

1. Not all adults have any idea how to sort out bullying.

2. Some adults make things an awful lot worse.

3. You are scared you'll get bullied even more for telling – even if you were totally in the right.

When you're a little kid, it's right, and important, that adults look after you and protect you.

As you grow up, I think what you really need are ways of sorting out most bullying stuff for yourself. It doesn't feel very empowering if every time there's a problem, you ask somebody else to sort it out for you, does it?

What we really, really need to know is:

- when it's OK to just let something go

- when it's something we can deal with ourselves

- when we absolutely need to get adults involved.

For example:

- A friend suggests you do something really stupid. You know they wouldn't normally mean it. You can probably safely just let this go.

- Someone you know but don't really trust suggests the same stupid thing. This is where having some ideas of how to respond to them, in a way that defuses the situation, would be really handy.

- What if the person suggesting you do it is an adult? In this case you definitely need to find a different adult, one you trust, and talk to them about it.

BULLIES HAVE NO FRIENDS!

Ooh, I so wish I had a £1 for every time I've heard this. *Absolute fake news.* And sometimes the bully is also actually supposed to be your friend...

IT'S NOT HOW YOU LOOK, IT'S WHAT'S INSIDE THAT MATTERS!

This is a tricky one. It's partly true. And partly fake news. I'll explain...

Our brains have evolved to spot a threat really fast. So, if someone looks very different from what you were expecting, your brain will register that too fast for you to even realise!

You can see that if someone looks different in any way – their face, their clothes, their behaviour, the way they talk – they are going to get more attention than if they looked just like you.

Suppose that person who gets spotted really fast is you. Would you enjoy all the extra attention? If you'd just done something amazing, maybe.

But what tends to happen is that all the attention, over time, becomes a negative thing. OK, people can't help feeling anxious around anyone who is different from them, but sometimes they are just horribly rude.

This is a major problem with things like racism. Different skin colour, different clothing. Two things that will get noticed. What about if you have a facial difference? Or get around in a wheelchair?

It's easy to see that all this negative attention, just because you look different, would be a major pain. And if people also look horrified or laugh, or give you the 'Oh, you poor thing!' stare, then maybe you'd either hide away or face the world with a scowl. Totally understandable.

What we're going to look at in the next chapter is how *the way you feel about yourself* also affects how people look at you. And how this can make a surprisingly big difference!

BULLYING STOPS WHEN YOU LEAVE SCHOOL!

I'm sorry. Whoever told you this was probably trying to be kind. But they were wrong.

Learning now how to cope with being (or just *feeling*) bullied is one of the most useful things you can do!

REVENGE IS THE ONLY WAY!

Actually, I found a really surprising thing when I asked young people what they wanted to happen after they got bullied.

Yes, lots said they wanted to get even.

And lots said they wanted the bully to be punished!

But the BIG thing that nearly everyone said was that they wanted to be popular.

Was this because they thought if you're popular you're less likely to get bullied? I think it probably was.

But it's important to realise here that getting revenge, and getting bullies punished, might not be the way to be popular.

So when I thought about, and experimented with, ways to cope with bullying so that you ended up feeling better about yourself, you can see this was quite a big thing to consider.

Are you beginning to understand now why you might find bullying so hard to sort out?

This book is here to show you how to deal with bullies and bullying so that when you leave school and start work, and get into relationships with other people, you will know…

Everyone feels bullied sometimes. But some deal with it much better than others.

It matters not one tiny bit whether you are someone who looks different, sounds different, thinks or behaves differently from that 'not average but still absolutely normal' measurement!

You can still be that person with a useful variety of successful strategies that you can practise now to make you more confident.

First one in the next chapter…

Chapter 3

HOW DO YOU DESCRIBE YOURSELF?

(AND DOES IT MATTER?)

As an idea, do you think that the way we look affects whether we get bullied or not? I'm really interested in what you think about this because I've done a lot of research on it.

Some autistics say they don't much care about the way they look. I care very much – but my thing is that I definitely don't want to look average. I *like* to look different. (And whatever I wear has to be comfortable because I can't bear scratchy labels, or seams, or wool, or nylon things. It makes me shudder even just *thinking* about them!)

But it would be interesting to look at this idea of 'the way you look affects whether you get bullied' scientifically. So, this anti-bullying strategy needs you to do an actual experiment.

Why? Because it's no good me just saying, 'Do this, because I think it works.' People say all sorts of things and give you no actual proof at all (this would be very bad science).

Background...

We see so many pictures of people looking amazing. This is really easy with a digital camera – you just delete any photo you look bad in. But looking at these photos can make us feel seriously inadequate about ourselves.

Most people only put up the photos in which they look good, are with their mates and are in interesting or fun places. Experiments have shown that our self-esteem goes down after seeing these sorts of photos. They are clearly much better-looking and more popular (less bullied) than we are. So it's easy for us to come to the conclusion that to be popular you have to look really good.

We could easily test this.

This is our hypothesis:

Good-looking people are more popular.

Method for testing if this is true...

I need you to imagine this is the worst day ever. (And if it IS your worst day ever, I'm really sorry and am sending you virtual hugs and a virtual slice of my finest lemon drizzle cake. I promise we *are* going to sort this out.)

Supposing you have an exam at school that you've forgotten to revise for.

And you get up late.

And your favourite school clothes are in the wash so now you've got the itchy ones you feel really uncomfortable in.

And a new spot has come up on your nose.

And your mum is really, *really* irritated with you for forgetting that exam...

What THREE negative words would you use to describe yourself?

If it was me, it would be something along the lines of I'm stupid, I'm ugly and nobody loves me (horrible things like that).

Right. Can you think about those sorts of things I've described like exams and being in trouble and 'wrong' clothes and spots…and imagine how YOU might feel and how those feelings might affect…

Your facial expression?

You could do this by looking in a mirror? Or you could do it with a friend and see how each other looks?

Is your head down? Is your mouth turned down at the corners? Or your jaw clenched? If I looked at you, would there be much eye contact? Are you looking fierce or totally miserable?

Your body language?

Are your shoulders hunched? Arms folded protectively over your chest? Hands balled into fists or clutched together?

The way you might now behave?

How might these negative feelings (mine were 'stupid, ugly, unloved') affect the way you behave? Do you just give up on the day (What is the actual point? I'm going back to bed) or go into school feeling really awful, convinced you'll fail the exam and everyone will laugh at you for the way you look? Does feeling this anxious send you into a spiral of behaviours that make you even later/even more likely to get into trouble?

Now I need you to decide:

- When you feel this way, are you likely to be more, or *less*, popular today?

- When you feel this way, are you less, or *more*, likely to get bullied?

- Does feeling this way make you feel better about the situation? Or *even worse*?

It definitely made me feel a lot worse. I'm sorry because it probably made you feel bad too...

I'm really sorry to have put you through that. So here is a much, MUCH nicer part of this experiment...

Now we're going to imagine that it's a fantastic, phenomenal, brilliant day!

You get notice in the post that you passed all your exams!

Your mum suggests this needs a celebration and you can invite your mate to the cinema, or hire a film you really want to see, *and* you get any meal of your choice! Or go to the sea for the day? Or stay on your laptop or read a book?

You choose the thing you'd like most!

For once you have exactly the clothes you want to wear and your hair/skin is behaving!

NOW what are you going to say to describe yourself?

Again, if it was me, with all this good stuff going on, I'd be feeling really pleased. I'd be saying something to myself like, 'I'm clever, I'm worthwhile and I look great!'

But how would *you* feel if all those great things I've described had just happened to you? I need you to really use your imagination here on how it feels to have everything going just perfectly for you!

Now what is your facial expression (again, check in the mirror or with a friend)?

Do you look smiley? Is your mouth turning up at the corners? Is it easier to give some eye contact? Is your head up instead of down?

And what about your body language now?

Are your shoulders looking relaxed? Have your arms dropped down from crossing your chest? Hands stopped being clenched or clutched together?

How about the way you behave when you're feeling good?

Are you more likely to go out and see people?
Do you feel more confident and able to tackle things a bit better?

And remembering all these positive things:

- When you feel this way, are you likely to be more, or *less*, popular today?

- When you feel this way, are you less, or *more*, likely to get bullied?

- Does feeling this way make you feel better about yourself as a person? Or *even worse*?

It definitely made me feel loads better about myself than before. I hope it did you too?

Do you remember what our **hypothesis** was?

Good-looking people are more popular.

I hope you can see that our **conclusions** are going to be along the lines of 'Actually it's not *being good-looking* that makes us more popular, it's *feeling confident about ourselves* that makes a difference to whether people like us!'

Because we've just seen that the way we feel about ourselves makes a major difference to how other people treat us.

It's so important I'm going to repeat it, loudly!

☆ **THE WAY WE FEEL ABOUT OURSELVES AFFECTS HOW OTHER PEOPLE TREAT US!**

People who feel bad about themselves tend to look less friendly, have anxious or aggressive body language, and behave in ways that make it harder to get to know them (so it's harder to like them).

So even though what they really want when they feel upset might be to have a friend, or even someone to just say something sympathetic, because they look grumpy, or fierce, we tend to keep away from them.

So, that's the main part of the experiment over. We just need to do one thing more...

Do you remember when we had the really horrible day and it made everything seem a whole lot worse and we felt less popular and really awful about ourselves?

In real life we couldn't just change that. It would still start off as a rubbish day. Late, disorganised, wrong clothes and in trouble...

Would it be possible to turn THAT sort of day around?

It seems impossible. But we are going to have a really good attempt at it because leaving it as it was – the worst day EVER – was really horrible and miserable. I felt mean putting you through it even to prove an important point.

Most (the *average*) teenagers gain most of their self-esteem/self-respect from three particular areas: a skill they have that they value; something they like about their personalities; and something they like about their appearance.

So, I want you to think of THREE things about yourself that are positive.

1. First! Something that you reckon you are fairly *good* at:
   - sports (swimming, football, rugby, martial arts, running, etc.)
   - academic subjects (reading, maths, history, foreign languages, etc.)
   - creative skills (thinking, art, making things, gardening, etc.)?

2. Next! Something you *like* about your personality.
   - Examples – smiley, friendly, hard-working, gentle, kind, brave, loving, knowledgeable, ambitious, amazing, brilliant, determined, fascinating, energetic, creative, gorgeous, clever, enthusiastic, generous, helpful,

imaginative, optimistic, positive, polite, quiet, relaxed, sensible, surprising, responsible, trustworthy, unique, worthwhile.

3. Finally! Something you like about the way you look (this is the hardest one because we can be so self-critical about it). Find anything you're pretty happy with. Your hair? Your eyes? Your knees? Your eyelashes? Strong arms or legs? Anything at all!

And now we're going to choose one of each to use on that day when nothing was going right. Because some days DO seem awful. But we can stop them being any worse than they have to be by using the most incredible thing we have – our brain!

I'm thinking what would be my three things for making this particular day more manageable, because as an autistic person I happen to be fairly disorganised, and wearing stuff I hate is, for me, really, REALLY difficult to ignore...

I'd probably try something like:

1. SKILL: I'm a creative thinker. (I might not have revised for this exam but I'm pretty confident

that I can think of some creative solutions to
some of the questions that the teacher might
have set.)

2. PERSONALITY: I'm polite. (I'm not going to
   manage full school uniform but equally I'm
   not going to blast into school and cause a
   scene. I can apologise profusely and ask if
   I can please explain my clothes/being late
   properly later.)

3. APPEARANCE: I *love* this old, baggy, soft
   non-uniform cotton jumper I've got on. (I do
   know I'm going to be in trouble for this! But it
   is PERFECTION!)

And does feeling Creative, Polite and Comfortable
make a difference to my day? Massively. MASSIVELY!
My pulse goes down, my brain re-engages, I can
breathe properly again. And I have more energy.

So now it's your turn to do the work... I still can't
change your awful day, but *you definitely can* now you
have the tools.

Think about each one.

Check out that list I gave you. Which positive things

are going to make the day seem more manageable so that you end up feeling quite pleased with yourself for coping, rather than despairing?

SKILL?

PERSONALITY?

APPEARANCE?

It takes work but it's brilliant when you get it and realise you can help yourself to feel a lot less bullied by stuff!

Obviously, your words will change according to what scary task you're about to do.

If I'm talking to teachers, for instance, I might use 'I'm an expert, I'm friendly and my shoes are *amazing*!'

And if I have to go shopping on a day when I don't want be with other people, I might use 'I'm organised, I'm brave and I've done my hair very carefully!'

And now you've learnt how, you can keep practising and add another thing to your skill set (because you are an incredible, clever, phenomenal being)!

This is a fantastic thing to have done in our quest to

cope successfully with getting bullied! I want to shout 'High five!' but then you might shake your head and say, 'Oh dear, Emily, NOBODY says that anymore.' So I won't. But I AM really proud of you for tackling that experiment!

- So now we know we may not be average but we *are* normal.

- We know there is a lot of fake news around bullying.

- We know how to change the way we feel about ourselves, even on a bad day.

Next chapter? We'll learn a rather startling anti-bullying strategy!

Chapter 4

HOW TO CALM DOWN SO YOU CAN THINK CLEARLY

Do you remember I said we'd learn an anti-bullying strategy for that fake news piece of advice 'Just ignore it and it'll stop'?

I do a really sneaky trick when I talk to adults about bullying. First, I ask them what they think a psychologist does and they answer with things like being a psychotherapist, and I say that can be useful for people with phobias like snakes or rats or spiders. (And I watch very, very carefully to see how they react to these particular phobias. There are always some people in the audience who do a sort of quick shudder when I say the word 'spiders'...)

And then, later, I ask them who thinks ignoring bullies is a good idea?

Lots of nodding and agreeing! Yes! Most think this is a *very* good idea.

So, I ask one person (who I spotted doing that shudder thing when I said spiders) to come and do an experiment with me, and they come onstage looking smiley and confident.

I produce a wooden box with holes in the lid...
I describe the enormous but completely harmless spider that's inside... I watch the look of sheer panic that comes over them...and then I ask them to just ignore this huge spider but stand facing me, their feet apart. I then ask them to just push their hands against mine!

I expect you can see where this might be going? They are so busy panicking about the spider in the box that they can't think about anything else!

So one of two things always happens.

Either I can push them over really easily (because they really, really want to run away)! Or sometimes they nearly knock *me* over (because they want to fight their way past me and get off the stage)!

I'm now much kinder and I explain that when we are stressed because something scary is happening (and feeling bullied can feel horribly scary), our brains are not functioning very well. All our energy is going into our hands (to fight) or legs (to run away – fast!).

So, what seems like a sensible, logical piece of advice... *just does not work!*

Obviously, we need to get our brains working again so that we can think clearly because it's not always possible to run away from threats like people saying mean things.

I show this poor, terrified adult a really simple way to get their brain working again. Try it yourself while I describe it. It's dead easy, honest!

The idea for this is that when you panic, not enough oxygen goes to your brain. We need to find a way to get it there...

First of all, what colour do you think of when you think of courage/bravery?

Loads of people seem to choose the colour red, but it's up to you. Whatever works for you is just fine. Fluffy pale pink? Bright sunshiny yellow? Sky blue? Deep turquoise sea green?

Stand with your feet apart, hands by your side.

Breathe in that colour, deep into your stomach. Feel it heating up your stomach.

Now breathe that strong colour out as if it's going down your legs…past your knees…through your feet… and through the floor. I want you to imagine that this outgoing breath of yours is growing huge, massive roots under the floor… Keep breathing out…keep going…keep making those roots till you run out of breath!

Your lungs will now take over and you will gasp in a huge breath!

NOW oxygen is getting to your brain and you can suddenly think more clearly!

When I do this experiment with the spider-fearing

adult, I now repeat the standing-and-pushing-against-my-hands exercise with them…and guess what? However hard I push against them, they push the same amount!

I haven't taken away that spider, but they are back in control of their fears. The look of amazement (and relief!) on their faces is fantastic.

They can't believe it could be so simple.

And then I admit that I am *terrified* of spiders and the box is empty… Luckily, so far no one has decked me for putting them through this!

But you can see what a powerful and easy thing it is to do.

In a way, all we're doing is behaving as if we are a tree in a huge gale. When we feel threatened, it's like a major storm in our heads. You can see that trees with huge roots are far less likely to fall over in that gale than trees with no roots!

So grounding yourself is one way to cope with a huge variety of stresses!

Can I ask you one favour?

Because you are not going to think of this strategy straight off if you're in a panic, you need to practise it lots so that when you *do* have a panic, it is second nature to ground yourself this way as fast as possible!

Essentially, when we feel grounded, we are not worrying about the past and we are not panicking about the future. We are exactly in the here and now.

And this means we can be logical rather than awash with negative emotions!

Good, isn't it?

I use this grounding exercise lots with people who are really anxious about exams.

Or performing on stage.

Or meeting new people.

Or going somewhere new.

Sometimes we combine it with those positive words we've learnt to use when things are not looking too good.

 When would *you* use it?

And just in case you are interested in *why* this works, rather than 'Just ignore it'...

It seems to me that most advice on bullying comes from adults who are not being bullied!

So, they come up with *logical* solutions that make sense on paper and are easy to say...

There are major problems with this because *we aren't just logical beings.* And *definitely* not when we feel we're being threatened/bullied!

Brains take up about 30 per cent of your oxygen. That's a LOT! And as humans evolved, their brains made sure they survived in the face of dangers – such as huge animals charging towards them – by taking some of that oxygen from their brains and pumping it into their arms and legs so they could fight it or leg it!

You've probably heard of the Fight or Flight response? This is Fight or Flight working well!

And if you're ever faced with a car speeding towards you, or someone chasing after you, then you can see that this would be a *brilliant* survival response!

(IMPORTANT: If this happens to you, it is NOT a good time to be standing still and grounding yourself! RUN!)

But Fight or Flight does NOT work brilliantly if that threat is something like psychological bullying (someone trying to mess with your mind with threats). Or if you're about to do something that you are really anxious about, like singing a solo or going to a party.

This is when it's perfect to ground yourself, get out of that scary mass of emotion, and think clearly.

Try it. Practise it when you only feel a bit anxious.

And then when you feel quite a bit more anxious.

And keep going! You are always going to come up against things that make you feel anxious. But knowing you have this grounding strategy up your sleeve is going to make you a whole lot more confident.

And it adds perfectly to:

- You may not be average but you are normal.

- You know what is true and what is fake news around bullying.

- You know that thinking three positive things about yourself (a skill you have, something you like about your personality and something you like about your appearance) changes your facial expression, your body language, the way you behave and the way others treat you, creating a more positive experience!

- And now you know that you can easily calm yourself when you begin to find things a little scary.

Fantastic! HIGH FIVE! (Stop it, Emily, we've already told you...)

In the next chapter, we'll look at other people and how *what we think about them* might make a difference in this anti-bullying quest.

Chapter 5

WHY ARE OTHER PEOPLE SO AWFUL?

If you are a teenager, there are going to be loads of times when you come up against things you don't see the point in.

Like your parents wanting you to do something that *does not remotely interest you*!

Or them setting rules that seem to make no sense. (You MUST be home by 10.30 even though everyone else is allowed out until 11.30. WHAT?!)

And teachers who decide to set loads of homework in the holidays...

They are just horrible people, right?

Nope, not true.

Other people are just like you. (Well, not *just* like you, obviously. You and I know you are a particularly nice person!) What I mean is that they are doing their best, in their own weird ways, to survive.

But it definitely looks as if they're not doing it in a way that seems either fair or kind!

And what you would really, *really* like is for them to behave reasonably and helpfully – because behaving the way they do is actually doing your head in.

If I asked you to *describe* this person who is upsetting you, what words do you think you would use?

Horrible? Mean? Unfair? Rude?

I bet you can think of loads!

(A fact: in the English language there are more negative words to describe people than positive words! No wonder it's easier to be negative about ourselves – and other people – than be positive!)

Do you remember how, when we could only think of

awful things about ourselves, it showed in our faces, our body language and the way we behaved?

And this changed the way people treated us?

What if, when we think bad things about others, this *still* shows in our faces and body language and the way we behave?

And affects how others treat us?

Let's have a go...

You were going over to a mate's house to play their new video game this weekend. You've wanted to play this game ever since it came out!

But you forgot to do your homework *again*...and your mum finds out.

Your mum now says you are grounded until after the weekend...

Tell me: what words do you think you might use to describe your mum right now? How angry would you feel about this mean, vindictive (this means having an unreasonable desire for revenge!) person who's wrecking the one nice thing you were looking forward to all week?

(*Really*? Ouch! We're talking the same mum that cooks your food and does your laundry and works at a boring job so you all have somewhere to live…)

Yep, *that* one because she *knows* going to play this new video game matters to you a lot. She *knows* grounding you is the one thing that will really upset you.

And if you think those things about her (I'm guessing it's something like, 'You are so unfair. You *deliberately* ruin the *one* thing I was looking forward to this week. You are so *old* and you have *no idea*. You don't care about me. I *hate* you!')…

Was I about right?

Thought so!

And how do you think thinking all these things affects your facial expression? Do you have a 'face like thunder'?

Is your body language showing total rage and despair?

Are you in a sulk? Storming up to your room? Slamming doors?

Fair enough! But how do you think that will affect your mum?

Will she come and find you and say, 'I can see you're upset and angry, so I'm giving in and you can go?' (You wish!)

Well, when you were little, she might have done.

But now she's faced with a teenager who's probably as big as her and is changing in quite scary ways all the time.

You are no longer her sweet little child who mostly did as they were told and kept saying things like, 'You're the best mum in the whole wide world!'

Can I tell you a secret? Most mums have mixed feelings about this.

- They want you to grow up and do great things!

- And they also really miss that mini you who behaved as if *she* was the most important thing in the world, rather than a new video game.

Complicated, isn't it?

So, sadly she's probably not going to give in. She's

angry too. She's tired of her job, she's mostly exhausted and she's desperate for you to do well at school so that you don't end up in a dead-end job like hers. She's putting in the extra hours so you can do well and you don't even bother to do your homework!!

And you didn't even say sorry! You just stormed off and she's now determined not to back down...(so now *she's* looking furious too).

This is not going to end well, is it?

It's upsetting me even as I'm imagining it!

You are going to have to do something really super-human here. Not easy but I have total confidence in you.

You are going to have to come up with THREE things about your mum that you really like and admire.

You'll find your own positive words for things that make sense to you in your family.

But what if it was something like 'She gives the best hugs, stands up for me when I'm not doing well, got me a dog when I really, badly wanted one...and now she looks after it because I keep forgetting'?

Even though you're still angry about the weekend, if you think *those* things, it changes your facial features. You stop looking aggressive. You probably smile remembering the hugs. And the time she made you chocolate brownies when you were really upset. And definitely the dog. Your body is not quite so tense, is it?

You can see she's probably not always unfair and mean and horrible! Maybe right now she's just really tired and upset?

And does that new thought affect the way you behave?

I'm really hoping – and expecting, if I'm honest – that it does!

Because recognising that others do not behave badly towards us because they hate us, *but because they're struggling themselves*, makes a massive, massive difference to how we handle situations that feel like bullying.

By the way...

It might not stop her saying no to going out this weekend, but going to find her and saying you're really sorry for forgetting your homework, and you'll do it tonight/try to be more organised in future because you understand why she thinks it's so important, is such a brilliant way to have a better, more adult relationship with her. It makes it more likely that she will trust you and enjoy your company as you grow more adult and do more and more things away from the safety of home.

Now, going back to the teacher who sets that extra holiday homework...

We all know which teachers we like most. They're the ones who help us to understand complex things and feel as if we'd like to know more.

And we all know the ones we *don't* like. The ones who just push us through stuff we don't even understand and get angry when we get it wrong.

The difficulty is that the education system is not exactly perfect. I need to explain this a bit because it's really useful to understand and often no one tells us these important things...

Schools are judged on how good their academic results are. The schools that get good GSCE and

A-level results are the ones that parents tend to choose for their kids.

They tend to be in areas where people have more money – bigger houses, more green spaces… And parents who can afford to put time and money into supporting the school.

Anyway, these schools that do well get more pupils. They can choose who goes there so they choose the brightest children (so they keep getting those good results).

The government gives schools money for every pupil they have on their books.

Because these academically more successful schools have all those extra pupils and that extra money that comes with them, they can afford to employ more specialist teachers. And more books. And more support staff. And repairs to the school buildings.

It becomes easier for them to get, and keep, their good results.

The schools that *aren't* doing so well academically often lose their best pupils (along with the money that comes with them from the government) to the schools that get better results.

These schools that lose pupils now have to cut staff. They lose their experienced staff first because they cost the most in wages.

And then the support staff have to go. So now teachers are teaching huge classes with no extra help for pupils who are struggling academically or behaviourally.

These pupils are less likely to be offered a place at the thriving school with lots of staff. They do not feel supported in the struggling school. They may end up staying off school or behaving badly. The school does its best but can't put in place all the things that would help because there is no spare money...

Not good, is it? You can now see that teachers are under a huge amount of pressure to get results, even though they probably went into teaching as a career because they wanted to inspire you!

They probably wanted to be the teacher that you, when you are older and famous, tell everyone about:

'I'll always remember this teacher because she inspired me to become the person I am today!'

I'm just saying all this because when I go into schools to work with classes, and talk about bullying, loads of classes say they feel bullied by their teachers.

We do a lot of work on understanding *why* teachers might seem like bullies (mostly because they're under a LOT of pressure to get those results).

And we talk about how we could change the way we think about them because hating them just doesn't seem to get us anywhere! They just get meaner!

I want you to know that I also talk to lots of teachers. I explain to them how the way they feel about their classes affects how their pupils behave!

After all, if they go into a lesson thinking, 'This is the worst class I teach all week!' how do you think that will affect how they teach you?

And how will YOU feel as a pupil? How might you react to them?

It becomes a battle. And then learning does not

happen. Nobody is feeling calm, breathing in lots of oxygen, thinking reasonably!

Everyone is stressed.

☆ **But it can change. There are things we can do.**

Here's one very useful exercise to use in school...

Being able to think of positive things about other people is related to a high IQ (those tests that people do to see how clever we are).

Because you clearly have a *high* IQ (meaning you are very clever), you can experiment with this for yourself.

Look around your classmates when you are next in school. When it's quiet and nothing much is happening – like waiting for the teacher to arrive.

Find ONE really positive word to describe each person. Something you would like to be said about you!

You'd be amazed at how often I've done this in classes and someone's come up to me after the class and said they'd never heard anyone *ever* say anything nice about them before! That's awful!

And I have to say, many, many teachers found this a really difficult exercise as well.

That's really sad. Please, please start finding those positive words! It changes:

- your facial expression

- your body language

- and the way you behave.

People are WAY more likely to start liking you.

You become a force for good.

The sort of person other people really want to get to know. Popular for all the right reasons!

Fantastic!

Keep practising!

The list's getting a bit long now but it's all good stuff!

- Not average but normal!

- Bullying statements – true or fake news?

- Feeling good about ourselves affects everything!

- Being grounded helps us think clearly rather than panic.

- Recognising that other people are, like us, trying to survive in their own ways helps us defuse difficult situations so that things are less horrible for everyone.

And the next chapter is about looking after your mental health...

Chapter 6

DEPRESSION...
AND WORSE

When you were really little, your brain was making all sorts of useful connections.

This person will feed me.

This sheet feels soft, that blanket feels scratchy.

If I hide my eyes, no one can see me. (I know!
But you've got to admit it's very sweet!)

When I smile, people like it and they smile back.

I am safe when I'm with these people.

That sort of thing. It all helps you survive in a very huge world.

Fast forward ten or so years and everything changes! Your whole brain decides to rewire itself so it can manage becoming an independent adult!

Nothing quite makes sense, everything seems strange. And your hormones play total *havoc* with your body. Which messes with your head as well.

It may well be a totally normal process, but honestly? I'm amazed *most* teens don't end up depressed.

The huge difficulties come when whatever it is that you're going through isn't supported by adults or the world at large.

When you look at the adult world you're about to enter, this is probably what you see:

- Everything is getting faster and faster (think about internet changes in even the last year!).

- Rich people are more likely to have power over our lives (more privately educated people get to the top in business and parliament than state-educated people).

- Everyone we see in films and on TV (think *Love Island*) seems to look good...

It's so easy to see that you might feel out of control. And downright frightened.

I truly feel for you. And I understand why, when you feel depressed, doing things like self-harming or eating too little or too much can seem like some sort of solution to numb the pain. Depression is a miserable thing. It makes quite awful things seem as if they might make sense.

The trouble is, all your emotions can feel overpoweringly strong. Whatever you feel just feels HUGE.

Add this to the fact that the part of your brain that *controls* all these emotions and decides what is risky behaviour (drinking alcohol or taking drugs, for instance) is not fully developed yet (in girls this part of the brain tends to be developed by the time they're around 20 but in boys it might not be until they're nearly 30!).

It's easy to see you might be taking what seem to adults to be huge risks and not even realise. And it can explain why adults sometimes seem to take over your control just when you feel you have very little. It may not always be done in what feels like a kind, sympathetic way. But they are now panicking and they're doing it to protect you.

I don't want to get into the whole 'Don't take drugs' argument. I know adults do it. And drink too much alcohol. And smoke.

I'm just saying the scientific evidence shows that teenage brains are *worse* affected, and for longer, than fully formed adult brains.

Nope, it's absolutely not fair. But it *is* a fact.

So, when you've got to this stage and you feel you are not coping with stuff at all, what do you do?

First off, talk to an adult you trust. Your parent or carer. A sympathetic relative. Your GP. A teacher. Just talking and having someone really listen might make all the difference.

Or they might suggest extra, professional help to get you through this bit.

Because when we feel depressed, the main thing we feel is isolated.

Completely on our own.

No one cares.

No one understands.

No one feels/has ever felt this hopeless and like such a failure.

It's a truly horrible feeling. I understand, I've been there. And I'm really, genuinely sorry you feel that way.

Because it feels like a different sort of bullying – like being bullied by life itself.

Since I can't offer a hug, or my famous lemon drizzle cake, I can at least offer you THREE strategies to help with this sort of feeling bullied. In their own ways, they all help you feel better about yourself and more back in control. Which is what you need right now.

1. KEEP A DIARY

Why would this help? Surely, writing down day after day how miserable you feel is going to make it all feel a lot worse?

Well, no! Oddly, when people (and I mean psychologists)

looked at how people cope best with feeling wretched, they found that those who wrote it all out – what happened, how they felt – actually got better from feeling depressed a lot quicker than the people who didn't keep a diary.

Try it? Please? You've got nothing to lose.

And for once it doesn't matter one tiny bit whether you spell well or have neat handwriting. No one will see what you've written except you.

Why might it have helped? Well, what reading back our diaries shows us is that it wasn't ALL bad. There were actually some good bits.

And that's really important because when we feel low, it can feel as if everything is bad the whole time.

There is a word for this if you're interested. It's called 'catastrophising' and it's when one bad thing feels like that means *nothing* is good.

When we are in really low spirits, we need reminding that they may be a bit thin on the ground right now, but there *are* good things happening as well.

And that means there is hope that things will improve.

They will get better. And we will feel OK again and have times when we are really happy.

2. KEEP A 'NICE THINGS' JAR

When you feel low, it's easy to not bother to do anything nice or enjoyable. And not be able to even think what you *do* enjoy.

So right now, grab an empty jar or bag.

Tear a sheet of paper into strips.

On each strip of paper write something you would usually enjoy doing.

Keep it simple! (For example, skiing makes me feel *very* happy…but on a hot day in July, it's not going to be possible, is it? But sitting in my garden with the cat and a cup of tea probably *is*!)

No one is judging you here. If the easy thing that makes you happy is talking to the dog, or watching *The Simpsons* on TV for the tenth time, write it down!

The point here is that when you are too miserable to think what you would even like, you have your jar to dip into and just do whatever comes up. (Which is why it has to be simple. Does that make more sense now?)

3. MEDITATING

Don't stop reading! I'm not going all spiritual on you!

But remember when we did the breathing and grounding exercise, way back in Chapter 4? Well, this is a bit like that, but for when you've got a few minutes spare and no one else is around.

This is for grounding your whole brain so it gets a bit of a rest from all that doom and gloom. Because getting stuck on any one thing is not very good for brains. They do best where there is a bit of difference. After all, if you only think one way, your brain makes more and more connections to that thing. Which means it can be harder and harder to think a different way.

If you need evidence of this, you just need to look at all those adults who can't seem able to understand basic facts like the earth is round! You can SHOW them the evidence in a video...but they stick firmly to what they've always thought – that the earth must be flat. It seems just too hard for them to accept that evidence because they've thought the wrong thing for such a long time.

So! How do you give your brain a rest?

Find somewhere fairly quiet (your bedroom?).

Set your phone to give you an alarm in two minutes.

Lie on the floor and just think about your breathing. Just breathe in...and out... That's it! You'll probably find after a minute your mind drifts off to other thoughts. Not a problem! That's absolutely normal. Gently bring it back again to thinking about your breathing.

I bet you'll find that two minutes went really, really fast!

Excellent. Could I ask you to do that two-minute exercise at least a couple of times a day? Maybe when you get up – I know, hardest time to find extra time for anything, but really important to set the day up better – then maybe after school, and even once more when you climb into bed at night?

You'll probably start finding pretty soon that you could actually manage a little bit longer. Don't rush it. Try five minutes for a while. Then maybe ten.

Personally, I'm OK now with 20 minutes in the morning and maybe ten minutes later if I feel I need it. I mostly work from home so that's pretty easy for me.

But you need to find what suits you best so that you can give that poor brain a rest from worrying and give it a bit of courage for the rest of the day.

If it helps, play some natural sounds (not music for this exercise – it's too distracting!) like the sound of rain or waves on a beach. There are meditation apps you can find on your phone that will do this for you.

So, those are three positive ways to cope with feeling really miserable and out of control that you can do for yourself.

They *don't* replace professional help, I know – sometimes this is exactly what you need – but with or without that, each of these three strategies gives you back some control over how you feel, and that's a major part of beginning to feel better again.

You *won't* be a teenager for ever.

Your hormones *will* settle down.

You *will* find your way as an adult.

It takes time and patience. And courage. And practice.

You can definitely do this. I'm right here, thinking of you and willing you on. Get help, believe in yourself – you are absolutely and totally worth it.

AND...I've got three more anti-bullying strategies for you in the very next chapter!

Chapter 7

THREE MORE USEFUL ANTI-BULLYING STRATEGIES

(USING HUMOUR, EXPLAINING, APOLOGISING)

The first anti-bullying strategies that we've done are the most important ones:

- understanding what bullying is

- understanding that how you feel about yourself – and how you feel about other people – has a big effect on how you end up getting treated

- being able to ground yourself...and just understanding that being a teenager is HUGELY EMOTIONAL.

The next two chapters of 'social skills' are the icing on the cake.

The more strategies you have under your belt, the more confident you will feel about ignoring the small, rubbish stuff, and being able to tackle the kind of bullying that really gets to you!

Remember the aim here is to *defuse* bullying behaviours (defuse means to make things less tense or dangerous).

This is because we now know that if somebody is trying to feel good about themselves by putting others down, just retaliating by putting *them* down will probably make them *even worse*...

I *know* it's hard not to just get your own back. I totally understand that urge to get even.

But lots of research by me and loads of others shows that this doesn't seem to stop the bullying. In fact, it actually seems to make it a *lot* worse...

So, what we're aiming for here is a sort of win-win situation.

- Someone is deliberately mean to you so they can shore up their shaky self-esteem.

- You use ways of dealing with this that make you both feel better about yourselves.

Result? They may well end up being nicer to you. And at least they are not going to get any worse!

1. USING HUMOUR

We've probably all heard of famous comedians who say they got bullied at school and found the only way out of it was to make people laugh.

In fact, I watched a comedian on TV last night saying he developed his really successful comedy skills because he got laughed at every day at school by a boy called David. 'But' – punchline coming up – 'he's now out of work and I'm here on TV! Who's laughing NOW, David?' Everyone in the audience laughed and cheered because it seemed as if the bully had finally got his comeuppance.

So, it seems like a sure-fire solution, right?

Major warning! The difficulty here is that what makes *you* laugh – and what makes me laugh – might be very, very different! (And I bet that if David watched that programme, he didn't laugh much!)

Being funny depends on two things.

1. Who is telling the joke?

2. Who is listening to them?

So, making a joke about a teacher being rubbish, to your mates, might have them cracking up.

But telling the same joke to a member of staff will probably end up with you in detention!

Same joke. Different audience! Makes a BIG difference!

So, yet another minefield to negotiate, isn't it?

I have often heard adults suggest using sarcasm as a joke.

It's bad advice.

It makes things a lot worse if what you're trying to do is make a bad situation less bad (defuse it).

For example, if somebody calls me a mad old bat

(I know! Shocking, isn't it?), I *could* turn around and say, 'Better mad and old than young and stupid!'

Is that going to defuse the bullying behaviour?

Nope, most probably not! It'll probably make a bad situation worse because I've called the other person stupid!

Sarcasm is only for people who are in power. They might find that humiliating others by poking fun at them is very funny. Apart from their mates, it's unlikely that anyone else enjoys this kind of put-down.

So how *do* we use humour to defuse an unpleasant situation?

Have you heard of the term 'self-deprecating humour'? It means *being able to laugh at yourself*.

Now I'm NOT suggesting you put yourself down all the time. That would not be at all good for your own self-esteem. But understanding that it can take the sting out of a stupid comment someone else said is a useful skill.

'How come you're so fat?' (*'Look, mate, it hasn't been easy! I've worked extremely hard to get to this shape!'*)

'You're a mad old bat!' (*'And a bit crazier with each passing year, mate!'*)

Regardless of your sexuality, it gets really boring hearing 'Why are you so gay?' followed by gales of sniggering laughter.

But working on that defusing response is always going to be worth your time and effort.

People laugh at things that make them anxious. Many kids are brought up by parents who have been taught that not being your average heterosexual is just wrong. It doesn't mean they're right; it just means they're anxious around possible differences.

Same goes for you if you're from another culture. People still get anxious around anything different from them.

Or if you look different.

Or behave differently.

People are just going to notice. And some are going to use *their* kind of humour (sarcasm) against you.

Practising ways of laughing it off without putting yourself down too much is a massive, massive skill for you to develop. It will be useful for the rest of your life in defusing really difficult and potentially threatening situations.

Important point: *Sometimes the 'humour' aimed at us is overpoweringly awful.* Not something you – or anyone else – should, or can, laugh off. In this case, do your best to walk away.

Because this is NOT humour that you're defusing – it's a hate crime, and it's definitely worth getting an adult involved. It's illegal and offensive.

2. HAVING AN EXPLANATION

If you are in any way different from the way the average person is around you, we've already understood that there is the likelihood that you'll get some really intrusive comments.

Not just once. But over, and over, and over.

Here, people aren't joking. They're asking a question

with a hidden agenda (something *they* know but they think you don't).

What they say (*and what their hidden agenda is*):

- 'What is the matter with you?' (*Why do you need a support worker?*)

- 'What happened to you?' (*Why do you so look different?*)

- 'Where are your parents?' (*Why don't your parents want you?*)

- 'But where are you *really* from?' (*Surely real Londoners are white?*)

All these (embarrassing) questions will have been heard *endlessly* by anyone who looks, sounds or behaves even slightly differently from what is 'average'.

The point, I'm sure you'll remember from earlier, is that difference makes people *anxious and confused*.

Sometimes it's a great deal easier to cope if you understand what they're getting at, and have a clear, brief explanation to hand!

So, while your first response is to perfectly reasonably ask, 'WHY?' (because you are entitled to know what it is that they're getting at), having a quick reply up your sleeve saves time and getting irritable being asked the same daft question for the twentieth time that week...

- 'What is the matter with you?'

  'I have a support worker because my brain is differently wired from yours. I'm good at some things but I really struggle with things like organisation, so my support worker helps with that so I can become more independent.'

- 'What happened to you?'

  'I was born with something called cerebral palsy. It doesn't affect my brain but it affects my breathing and how I move. That's why I use walking aids or a wheelchair.'

- 'Where are your parents?'

  'My parents weren't able to look after kids full time so for now I'm with foster carers.'

- 'But where are you *really* from?'

> 'My grandparents came here from The Gambia,
> 60 years ago, to work for the NHS. So, I've
> never been there, I've always lived here.'

Yep, people asking these questions irritates me too. I'm just suggesting ways to be reasonable that might just end those boring questions.

Of course, you *could* just say, 'Mind your own business!'

But that wouldn't defuse the situation and it wouldn't educate them.

And it's important to do that because many, many people have very narrow horizons and that's not useful for you – or any of us.

3. APOLOGISING

This technique is very helpful if you really aren't getting on with your parents or your teachers for some reason. For times when they're angry and you feel no one is listening to you.

I'll explain. Often when people are anxious about us,

they get angry. (Anger is a much easier emotion to cope with than anxiety for an awful lot of people.)

For instance…

You went to a party. Your folks knew you were going but weren't exactly sure *where* it was because *you* weren't sure. But your friends were going in a car and would definitely give you a lift back home.

Your folks said, very clearly, 'Be back by 11.30!'

I'm guessing here that you might have scowled or sighed heavily… No one else *ever* has to be back that early? I'll just put it out there that my parents expected me home by 10.30 right up until I left home to get married at 19! Aaaargh!

Anyway, this is about you. You went. The party was up a lane somewhere, and not even all that good. At 11.15 you were actually quite glad to be leaving. Rubbish music and hardly anyone you knew was there…

You went looking for the person who said they'd give you a lift. Two problems: first, you can't find them; second, there is no internet connection. You check

outside for the car you came in. Still can't find
the driver...

You can't let your parents know because there is no
internet.

You can't phone the driver because there is no internet.

Your parents at home can't track where you are
because you have no internet.

This is building nicely, isn't it?

When you *eventually* track down the driver, it is 2.30
in the morning. You've looked everywhere. You were
actually pretty worried. Even a bit scared. The party
was sort of over and you didn't know what you were
supposed to do except keep looking...

When you arrive back home it is nearly 3 o'clock.

You are safe and sound, so your parents are relieved
and happy, yes?

Nope. They've gone through every awful thing that
could ever have happened to you in their minds. Your
mum is probably in tears ('*Why* did we let her go?')
and your dad – who has had your mum weeping over

him from 11.35 – is really not a happy bloke because this wasn't a problem he could solve.

They explode.

'Where the *hell* do you think you've been?'

'That's it! You are grounded!'

'Clearly you cannot be trusted!'

'Your mother has been *beside* herself!'

'We have to work tomorrow morning while you can just lie in bed thinking of no one but yourself!'

I don't suppose I need to go on?

And you, who were quite nervous yourself, and tried really hard to get back, what do you say when faced with all this rage?

Most likely, 'God! You are so *unfair!*' or '*I hate you!*'?

My advice?

Understand that what people say in anger is very often a cover-up for their fright and anxiety.

Wait until they've got it off their chests and then apologise. Properly. It may not have been your actual fault, but these people are upset and were very frightened on your behalf.

If they'll listen, explain what happened or offer to tell them the next day because you can see they're too upset just now. Or write a letter explaining.

Yes, one day you'll leave home and you can do as you please. But in the meantime, these are people who care that you're safe and will put themselves out to make sure you're OK. Remember to be a bit grateful for that.

Same with teachers. Yes, we know they have to make sure you get decent marks so the school looks good. But I'm willing to bet that the reason they get mad when you forget your homework yet again is that they see you as somebody with potential. Somebody they would be pleased to see do well.

If you struggle with writing, or reading or understanding, find a moment to explain your difficulties to teachers.

Tell them you're really sorry that you don't seem to be doing as well as you should.

Then tell them why. Tell them the things you seem to find harder than your mates.

You'd think they might guess you found some things really hard, but the truth is they just learn how to teach big classes when they're at college. Sadly, mind-reading classes are very, very rare at teacher training colleges...

If you explain what you find difficult, there is at least a chance that they'll be able to find a way around it, to help. (Because they do teach THOSE classes at teacher training colleges.)

Essentially, this anti-bullying strategy is about recognising that emotions are very powerful and not logical. Being able to see what the emotion is behind the statement makes it possible for you to sympathise and then explain your logic.

Again, it defuses a difficult situation.

Again, it takes practice and courage.

Again, it's win-win.

Chapter 8

LAST FOUR STRATEGIES!

(SAYING NO, DISTRACTION, CLOTHES, FRIENDS)

Phew! I can't believe we're nearly at the end! I shall miss thinking about you when I stop writing this book, because I have a really clear image of you in my mind. I'm hoping that you're thinking, 'I could do all this stuff!' and 'Why did no one tell me this before?'

Because you are a teenager, you are doing your level best to manage school, parents, friends and growing up.

And there are times when it all seems way too much and way too confusing!

And this is why I'm writing this book for you (and why you're reading it).

1. SAYING NO

Why, when people ask us to do stuff that we know is going to overload us, or we don't even like, do we still say 'Yes' even when our brain is saying '*No!*'?

'Come to this party!' (*Aaargh! I definitely don't want to go. I hate parties!*) 'Yeah, OK!'

'Try this drug/drink/food!' (*Why? I don't actually want to!*) 'Oh, OK, just this once!'

'Can I copy your homework again?' (*Really? Again? No!*) 'Yep, no problem!'

Crazy, isn't it?

But we all do it because somehow it seems we'll offend others if we don't agree. We feel a bit desperate to be liked and to fit in.

This is probably because all our lives our families and communities have stressed how important it is to fit in.

You know you have to say please and thank you. And kiss Granny even if she smells a bit.

You know you have to wait your turn in a conversation or everyone gets mad at you interrupting all the time (though I'm not sure all politicians have learnt this!).

You know if you 'behave' now, you're likely to get a treat afterwards.

And equally you know that running out into a road without looking can have very serious consequences for both you and the driver of the car coming along the road.

All these things we learn (are taught) early on because it's in our family's or community's interests that we follow some basic safety and social rules.

This means we are more likely to be accepted by others, and also we are more predictable, so folk don't have to keep on nagging us to 'Say *please*!'

Mostly it makes it easier for everyone.

Until you are out on your own. Where the urge to fit

in with a different group – the people you think of as your peers – comes in...

Then you are still remembering that for people to actually *like* you (I'm not talking about loving you – even very inadequate parents love their kids), you feel you have to do as they ask...

Then it's not useful, is it?

Then you have to learn the lesson that families often forget to teach you. *How to say NO.*

And how to say it in a way that doesn't upset the other person too much – especially as it's probably one of your friends.

Just saying 'No thanks! That's not for me!' would be fantastic. If you can do this, you are way ahead of me. Excellent stuff.

But if you find it really hard to be that straight (and a lot of us do), then here are some suggestions of what you could say – but keep thinking of other things too because all our lives people ask us to do things that upset us, exhaust us, bore us or just scare us.

'Sorry, I'm doing something else that night.'

'Not this time.'

'Thanks for asking, but no.'

'Can I take a rain check on that, please?'

'I can't take on anything else right now.'

'That doesn't work for me.'

'Oh look! A squirrel!' (This is an in-joke with autistics because we are liable to go off at a tangent like this just when you thought we were listening really hard. We're easily distracted!)

But it is a perfect example of getting out of saying yes, and it leads me neatly into the next technique!

2. DISTRACTION

This is just a handy way of putting someone off their stroke.

For instance...

I nearly always wear big, chunky necklaces. So, to demonstrate this technique of distraction, if I'm working with a class in school, I ask somebody to chuck an insult at me.

They all look a bit worried, then one person (nearly always a boy) will say something like 'Why have you got a string of tomatoes round your neck, Miss?' (and, mostly, everyone else laughs nervously!).

First, I answer back the way anyone who wasn't interested in defusing a situation might: I reply, 'And why do you look such an idiot?' (Yep, I know this was unfair since I *asked* him to insult me. Bear with me a minute...)

I ask him if this will defuse the situation and we can be friends?

'NO!'

So I ask the poor chap to do exactly the same thing again – 'Why ARE you wearing that stupid big necklace?'

This time I use distraction.

I ask when break time is in this school. And *every single time* the response is along the lines of 'It's at 11 o'clock, Miss!'

You can see that distracting somebody when they're either about to tease you, or even after they have done, is one way to get out of it.

People can, and do, say daft and stupid things all the time. If we want to defuse the situation so that it's safer for us, then try distraction!

The important point here is that you are *ignoring* an attempt to wind you up because you and I know people can say stupid things. What you are *not* doing is ignoring the person who said it! This way they have your attention – which is what they wanted in the first place – but you've let them off the hook and, better still, you come out of it in a positive way with nobody (especially you) getting hurt!

And while we're on this subject of distracting, can I also suggest that, occasionally, flattering someone by giving them a compliment is also a great way to avoid being in trouble?

Because even if it embarrasses us a bit, we *all* like to have a real, genuine compliment.

Someone taking the time to notice that we got something right. Or that we took particular trouble with something. Or we look good. It makes us feel better about ourselves. We even smile more!

So, if you are finding somebody a pain at the moment, thinking of something genuinely kind to say is a fabulous way to defuse a scratchy relationship!

It is a PERFECT strategy to use when your mum comes into your room demanding that you take every used plate and mug to wash up (WHAT?).

'Thanks for the food, Mum, it was really great!' might not stop her from insisting that plates are not left to go mouldy under your bed. But she will know that you value her and what she does for you. And that helps defuse an awkward situation from just turning into another pointless argument about how often stuff needs washing up, especially now the dog has licked most of it pretty clean...

Teacher being angry with you for talking in class? Obviously, you're going to say sorry first of all. But then try saying something nice – 'It was a really interesting lesson, Miss/Sir' – and you will defuse the situation from getting any worse.

So that's another really useful strategy under your belt!

3. THE WAY YOU DRESS

Part of that fitting in that people try to do is to wear similar things.

Some of us follow every fashion.

Some of us wear a particular kind of clothing (mostly black and purple for Goths, mostly lycra for sporty people)...

And some wear a sort of uniform (jeans, T-shirt and hoodie) rather than have to think of something different to wear every day!

All these choices are great. Whatever suits you and you're comfortable in! Wearing certain stuff can make us feel part of a group.

But what you need to remember is that if what you wear is different from what *most* of your group are wearing, it will get noticed. That's definitely not a *bad* thing. I'm just letting you know in case you weren't sure already.

If you are desperate to fit in at all costs, you could always adapt what you want to wear a bit?

Especially in a new situation, it's sometimes a useful strategy to make you feel more confident.

For instance...

If I'm talking to groups of younger people, I'll wear whatever I'm comfortable in (probably jeans and T-shirt).

If I'm talking to a room full of teachers, I'll probably wear something fairly smart.

Why?

Because we notice. And even though we may change our minds later about someone, those first impressions do actually matter.

So, if you ever have to go to court (I hope not, but you might one day), make sure you look really quietly and smartly dressed because people judge you as a person, based on how you look, in less than *two seconds*!

Same if you have to go for an interview.

Same if you want to impress someone you fancy.

No one, and definitely not me, is suggesting you spend your life in uncomfortable things that you hate!

Part of what makes you is the way you choose to look. It makes you individual and interesting!

I'm just pointing out that we all look at others and make snap judgements. You don't need to change but it's extremely useful to be aware of it.

4. AND LAST, BUT DEFINITELY NOT LEAST, FRIENDS!

I guess this is a really obvious anti-bullying strategy because most of us know that we're better off in a group than sticking out as a 'sad loner'.

Not only are we less likely to get picked on if we're in a group, but we also get that group's support.

Sadly, when you feel bullied, you are actually *less* likely to seek out your friends. Being bullied knocks your self-esteem and you feel that probably everyone is laughing at you now or doesn't care that you're upset. Suddenly, you are *less* likely to want to go out with mates and do the things you usually enjoy. Double disaster really.

Time to work really hard on those feelings of self-worth that we looked at in Chapter 3.

Remember your skills, the things you value about your personality, the bits about your appearance that you reckon are OK.

Work on saying these positive things about yourself under your breath before you leave home each day. Just to remind yourself that you are way more than just 'someone who happened to get bullied'.

Then re-join your mates. Without starting a war (telling the story in a way that makes you look good and the bully look completely vile), just say you were upset by some comments and you're working on it.

That way, you're still part of the friendship group. Which is important. If you've been bullied, you *need* to have friends around you to support you.

And finally, what about if you find it difficult to make friends in the first place?

The secret to this is to think about what really interests you and then find people who are interested in the same things! Then there is always something to talk about! (Not everyone is interested in football or boy bands or clothes. Some of us love trains or wildlife or climbing mountains.)

Get out there and find your group! It might not be easy, but keep searching. Being part of a community – something bigger than you – is really good for your mental health!

You could follow your hobbies doing local stuff. Join a drama group or a choir? Or a band? Or chess group? Or skateboarding?

You could volunteer to visit somebody elderly or housebound.

Or help a busy mum once a week by taking her kids to the park.

You could be part of a national movement like the Guides or Scouts.

You could do a Duke of Edinburgh award.

You could be part of a huge international movement, fighting for big changes like slowing down the climate crisis.

Or join societies that fight for equal rights for those who have difficulties of one sort or another.

If you aren't sure where to start, have a look online!
Or ask someone! Anyone! JUST DO IT!

AND LAST OF ALL...

First off, I need to remind you of some stuff...

- It is SO not your fault if you get bullied by people who have learnt negative ways to feel good about themselves. But you don't need to join them. We can all do our bit by understanding bullying and defusing situations where we can (so that we make the world a bit nicer and a bit kinder for everyone – including ourselves).

- We can now see that feeling good about ourselves and having more understanding of where other people might be coming from, is really helpful for improving our self-esteem.

- We've got some really good calming strategies sorted to practise and use for the rest of our lives, to improve our mental health.

- We now understand some of those unwritten

social things that nobody thinks to tell you because they assume everyone knows (only we didn't!).

• We have a whole list of good things we can use for ourselves *and* that we can explain to others if *they* get bullied.

Next, I need to remind you that at the end of the book there is a list of extra resources that you might find useful – other books you could read and other organisations you might find helpful (because nobody knows everything!).

And last of all I need to say cheerio. Which fills me with lots of different emotions, all at the same time, which is a bit confusing.

I feel sad because all the time I'm typing this I'm thinking about you, and when I stop, I'm going to miss you. So, you know, hugs and all that.

And at the same time, I'm thinking how chuffed I am that you read all the way through and now you have a whole stack of things to make your life a lot easier and more understandable, and how brilliant that is.

So, HIGH FIVE! (I don't even care anymore, I'm that happy for you!)

And you can always let me know how you're doing. My website is: www.thebullyingdoctor.com and there's a list of useful organisations at the end, which includes contact details.

So...GOOD LUCK! xxx

EXTRA RESOURCES YOU MIGHT FIND HELPFUL

BOOKS YOU MIGHT LIKE

Blame My Brain: The Amazing Teenage Brain Revealed by Nicola Morgan (Walker Books, 2005) – loads of info on teenage brains and what causes you to behave the way you do!

Teen Esteem: A Self-Direction Manual for Young Adults by Dr Pat Palmer and Melissa Alberti Froehner (3rd Edition, Impact Publishers, 2010) – this is probably for older teens but has lots of useful stuff on negotiating the adult world.

Why Your Parents Are Driving You Up the Wall and What To Do About It by Dr Dean Burnett (Penguin, 2019) – he's a neuroscientist who writes really interesting stuff about brains that makes you laugh at the same time as learning loads.

Freaks, Geeks and Asperger Syndrome: A Useful Guide to Adolescence by Luke Jackson (Jessica Kingsley Publishers, 2002) – an autistic teenager in an autistic family.

My Hidden Chimp by Prof Steve Peters (Studio Press, 2018) – imagining how that evolutionary bit of your brain can sometimes mess with what is expected of you!

Autism and Asperger Syndrome in Children by Dr Luke Beardon (Sheldon Press, 2019) – this is aimed at adults so could be a hard read, but it's really good on the positives of autism and how we survive best.

The State of Grace by Rachael Lucas (Macmillan Children's Books, 2017) – a fantastic novel about an autistic girl called Grace.

ORGANISATIONS THAT MIGHT BE USEFUL

Samaritans

This is a resource for anyone who is not feeling OK about life, and you can contact them in various ways. They're there for you 24/7.

By free phone: 116 123 or online: jo@samaritans.org.

They have a website – www.samaritans.org.

Childline

They have lots of info online on things like money, relationships, gambling and depression. They've also got ways of dealing with feeling unhappy like 'Build your happy place', 'Wall of Expression' and 'Balloon'.

You can have a 1-2-1 counsellor chat via their website www.childline.org.uk or you can phone them for free – 0800 1111.

If you are LGBTQ+

Stonewall Youth have loads of info on different sexualities on their website www.youngstonewall.org.uk. Useful information here on health and well-being and coming out.

Eating disorders?

Beat have a specialist Youthline phone number: 0808 801 0711.

www.beateatingdisorders.org.uk

This site describes different kinds of eating disorders and gives you advice on how to talk to your GP about your eating worries so that you can get some help.

For general mental health worries

Mind's website www.mind.org has loads of information and help on your feelings and talking to your GP and your parents about them so that they can understand. You can phone them free on 0300 123 3393 or you can chat to them online from the website.

National Autistic Society

This is the organisation for specific queries about being autistic, with recommended books and groups for teens. You can find them at www.autism.org.uk.

Self-harm worries?

Mind has a section on self-harm on their website

www.mind.org. You can phone them free on
0300 123 3393 or text 86463.

And last but not least
Frank – www.talktofrank.com – has really useful
advice and help on drugs. You can phone them free on
0300 1236600 or text 82111.

These aren't the only websites, but looking through
them, these seem the safest and most helpful for
people your age.

of related interests

The Spectrum Girl's Survival Guide
How to Grow Up Awesome and Autistic
Siena Castellon

Paperback: £12.99 / $18.95
ISBN: 978 1 78775 183 5
eISBN: 978 1 78775 184 2
256 pages

"Never be ashamed of being different: it is this difference that makes you extraordinary and unique."

This essential go-to guide gives you all the advice and tools you'll need to help you flourish and achieve what you want in life. From the answers to everyday questions such as 'Am I using appropriate body language?' and 'Did I say the wrong thing?', through to discussing the importance of understanding your emotions, looking after your physical and mental health and coping with anxiety and sensory overloads, award-winning neurodiversity campaigner Siena Castellon uses her own experiences to provide you with the skills to overcome any challenge.

With practical tips on friendships, dating, body image, consent and appearance, as well as how to survive school and bullying, *The Spectrum Girl's Survival Guide* gives you the power to embrace who you are, reminding you that even during the toughest of teen moments, you are never alone.

Siena Castellon is a 17-year-old internationally recognised and multi-award-winning autism advocate and anti-bullying campaigner who is on the autism spectrum. She has won a BBC Radio 1 Teen Hero Award, *Observer* New Radical Award and the British Citizen Youth Award and is affiliated with the UCL Centre for Research in Autism and Education. She lives in London with her parents and her pet dog Rico.

Getting the Best Out of College for Students on the Autism Spectrum
A Workbook for Entering
Further Education
Kate Ripley and Dr Rebecca Murphy

Paperback: £14.99 / $20.95

ISBN: 978 1 78775 329 7

eISBN: 978 1 78775 330 3

160 pages

Thinking about going to college? What subjects to take? How to organise your time properly? How to meet new people and maintain friendships?

This interactive workbook provides guidance for your entire journey through college and further education. Full of handy tips and strategies to help you through college, it guides you through early hurdles such as preparing for a new sensory environment, planning your transport and making friends. Chapters also cover life in college, so you'll know how to properly manage your time studying and socialising, how to get a grip on social media and have the confidence to tackle exams head on!

The book includes 100 pages of interactive elements, which develop decision-making, reflection and strategy-building skills, and you can work through it all with an older adult for help.

Kate Ripley is a Consultant Specialist Psychologist for Autism. She has worked as a Senior Specialist Educational Psychologist for Autistic Spectrum Disorders for Children's Services and is an author of nine books including *Autism from Diagnostic Pathway to Intervention, Exploring Friendships, Puberty and Relationships*. She lives in Devon.

Dr Rebecca Murphy is a Senior Educational Psychologist (EP) for the Isle of Wight, and has worked at Hampshire and Isle of Wight Educational Psychology since 2013. She is currently part of a working group leading EP involvement for further education providers. She lives in Hampshire.

Know Your Spectrum!
An Autism Creative Writing
Workbook for Teens
Finn Monahan

Paperback: £18.99 / $27.95

ISBN: 978 1 78592 435 4

288 pages

Not everyone with autism is the same. This workbook will help teenagers recognise their own individual spectrum of autistic behaviours, and reflect on the specific challenges they face, their own strengths and how they relate to other people.

Using creative writing activities, this book helps teenagers to identify connections between events and their emotions - which can be difficult for people with autism - while improving their writing skills through fun activities. A range of examples of poetry and short stories are included to make each activity accessible to all levels and to show how writing narrative and poems can help support personal reflection.

The book encourages the reader to explore the core aspects of autism including social communication, executive function, and sensory processing, and then allows the teen to create a template of their own spectrum of abilities within autism. This unique understanding of autism can then be used to develop individual strategies and encourage self-advocacy. Using this book collaboratively with teachers or parents means the teen can be supported in a way that is specific to them.

Finn Monahan is a specialist SPLD teacher working as a freelance Asperger's/Dyslexia Tutor and Disability Needs Assessor at Queen's University Belfast and the University of Ulster. She received a late diagnosis of Asperger's aged 38 and the impact of growing up without a diagnosis inspired her to write this book.

The Asperger Teen's Toolkit

Francis Musgrave

Paperback: £12.99 / $19.95

ISBN: 978 1 78592 161 2

eISBN: 978 1 78450 438 0

136 pages

Dealing with the everyday realities facing teens with Asperger Syndrome, this book presents a toolkit of tried-and-trusted ideas to help them work through difficulties and find the solutions that work best for them.

This book covers everything they need to know to thrive in their adolescent years, including how to hack your own internal alarm system to overcome anxiety and other difficult emotions.

It also arms teenagers with everything they need to navigate sexuality and relationships, develop a healthy self-image, deal with bullies, be smart with money and stay savvy online... In short, no issue is left unexplored.

Fun and informative, this is a must-read for teens with high-functioning autism, and for those who want to understand what adolescence is like on the spectrum.

Francis Musgrave is the author of *The Asperger Children's Toolkit*. He founded AS Active, a social enterprise supporting families of children with autism and Asperger Syndrome.

Freaks, Geeks and Asperger Syndrome
A User Guide to Adolescence
Luke Jackson

Paperback: £13.99 / $22.95
ISBN: 978 1 84310 098 0
eISBN: 978 1 84642 356 7
216 pages

Have you ever been called a freak or a geek? Have you ever felt like one?
Luke Jackson is 13 years old and has Asperger Syndrome. Over the years
Luke has learned to laugh at such names but there are other aspects of
life which are more difficult. Adolescence and the teenage years are a
minefield of emotions, transitions and decisions and when a child has
Asperger Syndrome, the result is often explosive.

Luke has three sisters and one brother in various stages of their
adolescent and teenage years but he is acutely aware of just how
different he is and how little information is available for adolescents
like himself.

Drawing from his own experiences and gaining information from his
teenage brother and sisters, he wrote this enlightening, honest and
witty book in an attempt to address difficult topics such as bullying,
friendships, when and how to tell others about AS, school problems,
dating and relationships, and morality.

Luke Jackson is 13 years old and has three sisters and three brothers.
One of his brothers has AD/HD, one is autistic and Luke has Asperger
Syndrome. He is the author of *A User Guide to the GF/CF Diet for Autism,
Asperger Syndrome and AD/HD*, also published by Jessica Kingsley
Publishers.